HEAL YOUR BODY

The Mental Causes
for Physical Illness
and the Metaphysical Way
to Overcome Them

LOUISE L. HAY

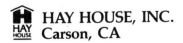

HAY HOUSE, INC.
Carson, CA

HEAL YOUR BODY

Hay House, Inc.
P.O. Box 6204
Carson, CA 90749-6204

The author of this book does not dispense medical advice nor prescribe the use of any technique as a form of treatment for medical problems without the advice of a physician, either directly or indirectly. The intent of the author is only to offer information of a general nature to help you cooperate with your doctor in your mutual quest for health. In the event you use any of the information in this book for yourself, you are prescribing for yourself, which is your constitutional right, but the author and publisher assume no responsibility for your actions.

Heal Your Body—Printing History
First Manuscript Printing, *What Hurts*, May,1976
First through Fourth Printings, *Heal Your Body*, Second Edition, 1978-1983
(ISBN 0-87418-05-5)
Fifth Through Twelfth Printings, New Revised Version, Third Edition, 1984-1987
(ISBN 0-937611-00-X)

Twenty-Ninth Printing, Fourth Edition (Expanded/Revised), April 1995

95 96 97 98   32 31 30 29

DEDICATION

I have long believed the following: "Everything I need to know is revealed to me." "Everything I need comes to me." "All is well in my life." There is no new knowledge. All is ancient and infinite. It is my joy and pleasure to gather together wisdom and knowledge for the benefit of those on the healing pathway. I dedicate this offering to all of you who have taught me what I know: to my many clients, to my friends in the field, to my teachers, and to the Divine Infinite Intelligence for channeling through me that which others need to hear.

Louise L. Hay

ACKNOWLEDGEMENTS

I wish to acknowledge Robert Lang, M.D., Associate Professor of Medicine, Yale University; Pete Grim, D.C.; and René Espy, D.C.; who all shared their ideas and wisdom with me.

FOREWORD TO THE
FOURTH EDITION

Little did I know when I first wrote the original version of *Heal Your Body* that today I would be writing a foreword to the fourth revised and expanded edition. The "little blue book," as it is so affectionately called by thousands, has become an indispensible item to many. I have sold hundreds of thousands of copies, far beyond my vision in the early days. *Heal Your Body* has opened countless doors, created friends for me everywhere. Wherever I travel, I meet people who show me well-worn copies carried constantly in their purses or pockets.

This little book does not "heal" anyone. It does awaken within you the ability to contribute to your own healing process. For us to become whole and healthy, we must balance the body, mind and spirit. We need to take good care of our bodies. We need to have a positive mental attitude about ourselves and about life. And we need to have a strong spiritual connection. When these three things are balanced, we rejoice in living. No doctor, no health practitioner can give us this unless we choose to take part in our healing process.

You will find many new additions in this version and it is also cross-referenced to provide more input. I suggest you make a list of every ailment you have ever had and look up the mental causes. You will discover a pattern that will show you a lot about yourself. Select a few of the affirmations and do them for a month. This will help eliminate old patterns you have been carrying for a long time.

Louise L. Hay

Santa Monica, CA
February 1, 1988

*Revised and Expanded Edition, April 1988

INTRODUCTION

In this newly-revised edition, I want to share with you one of the reasons I KNOW that dis-ease can be reversed by simply reversing mental patterns.

A few years ago, I was diagnosed as having cancer of the vagina. With my background of being raped when I was five years old and being a battered child, it was no wonder I had manifested cancer in the vaginal area. Having already been a teacher of healing for several years, I was very aware that I was now being given a chance to practice on myself and prove what I had been teaching others.

Like anyone who has just been told they have cancer, I went into total panic. And yet I knew that mental healing worked. Being aware that cancer comes from a pattern of deep resentment that is held for a long time, until it literally eats away at the body, I knew I had a lot of mental work to do. I realized that if I had the operation to get rid of the cancer and did not clear the mental pattern that created it, then the doctors would just keep cutting Louise until there was no more Louise to cut. If I had the operation and cleared the mental pattern that was causing the cancer, then the cancer would not return. When cancer or any other illness returns, I do not believe it is because the doctor did not "get it all out," but rather the patient has made no mental

1

changes and so just recreates the same illness. I also knew if I could clear the mental pattern that created the condition called cancer, I would not need the doctor. So I bargained for time. The doctor grudgingly gave me three months, at the same time warning me that my life was endangered by the delay.

I immediately began to work with my own teacher to clear old patterns of resentment. Up to that time, I had not acknowledged that I harbored deep resentment. We are often so blind to our own patterns. A lot of forgiveness work was in order. The other thing I did was to go to a good nutritionist and completely detoxify my body. So between the mental and physical cleansing, in six months I was able to get the medical profession to agree with what I already knew; that I no longer had any form of cancer. I still keep the original lab report as a reminder of how negatively creative I could be.

Now when a client comes to me, no matter how dire their predicament seems to be, I KNOW if they are WILLING to do the mental work of releasing and forgiving, almost anything can be healed. The word "incurable," which is so frightening to so many people, really only means that the particular condition cannot be cured by "outer" methods and that we must GO WITHIN to effect the healing. The condition came from nothing and will go back to nothing.

THE POINT OF POWER IS IN THE PRESENT MOMENT

Right here and right now in our own minds. It does not matter how long we have had negative patterns, or an illness, or a rotten relationship, or lack of finances, or self-hatred, we can begin to make a change today. The thoughts we have held and the words we have repeatedly used have created our life and experiences up to this point. Yet, that is past thinking, we have already done that. What we are choosing to think and say, today, this moment, will create tomorrow and the next day, and the next week and the next month and the next year, etc. The point of power is always in the present moment. This is where we begin to make changes. What a liberating idea. We can begin to let the old nonsense go. Right now. The smallest beginning will make a difference.

When you were a tiny baby, you were pure joy and love. You knew how important you were, you felt you were the center of the universe. You had such courage, you asked for what you wanted, and you expressed all your feelings openly. You loved yourself totally, every part of your body, including your feces. You knew you were perfect. And that is the truth of your being. All the rest is learned nonsense and can be unlearned.

How often have we said, "That's the way I am," or, "That's the way it is." What we are really saying is that it is what we "believe to be true for us." Usually what we believe is only someone else's opinion we have accepted and incorporated into our own belief system. It fits in with other things we believe. If we were taught as a child that the world is a frightening place, then everything we hear that fits in with that belief, we will accept as true for us. "Don't trust strangers," "Don't go out at night," "People cheat you," etc. On the other hand, if we were taught early in life that the world is a safe and joyous place, then we would believe other things. "Love is everywhere," "People are so friendly," "Money comes to me easily," and so on. Life experiences mirror our beliefs.

We seldom sit down and question our beliefs. For instance, I could ask myself, "Why do I believe it is difficult for me to learn? Is that really true? Is it true for me now? Where did that belief come from? Do I still believe it because a first-grade teacher told me over and over? Would I be better off if I dropped that belief?"

Stop for a moment and catch your thought. What are you thinking right now? If thoughts shape your life and experiences, would you want this thought to become true for you? If it is a thought of worry or anger or hurt or revenge, how do you think this thought will come back to you? If we want a joyous life, we must think joyous thoughts. Whatever we send out mentally or verbally will come back to us in like form.

Take a little time to listen to the words you say. If you hear yourself saying something three times, write it down. It has become a pattern for you. At the end of a week, look at the list you have made and you will see how your words fit your experiences. Be willing to change your words and thoughts and watch your life change. The way to control your life is to control your choice of words and thoughts. No one thinks in your mind but you.

4

MENTAL EQUIVALENTS:
The Mental Thought Patterns That Form Our Experience

Both the good in our lives and the dis-ease are the results of mental thought patterns which form our experiences. We all have many thought patterns that produce good, positive experiences, and these we enjoy. It is the negative thought patterns that produce uncomfortable, unrewarding experiences with which we are concerned. It is our desire to change our dis-ease in life into perfect health.

We have learned that for every effect in our lives, there is a thought pattern that precedes and maintains it. Our consistent thinking patterns create our experiences. Therefore, by changing our thinking patterns, we can change our experiences.

What a joy it was when I first discovered the words *metaphysical causations*. This describes the power in the words and thoughts that create experiences. This new awareness brought me understanding of the connection between thoughts and the different parts of the body and physical problems. I learned how I had unknowingly created dis-ease in myself and this made a great difference in my life. Now I could stop blaming life and other people for what was wrong in my life and my body.

I could now take full responsibility for my own health. Without either reproaching myself or feeling guilty, I began to see how to avoid creating thought patterns of dis-ease in the future.

For example, I could not understand why I repeatedly had problems with a stiff neck. Then I discovered that the neck represented being flexible on issues, being willing to see different sides of a question. I had been a very inflexible person, often refusing to listen to another side of a question out of fear. But, as I became more flexible in my thinking and able, with a loving understanding, to see another's viewpoint, my neck ceased to bother me. Now, if my neck becomes a bit stiff, I look to see where my thinking is stiff and rigid.

REPLACING OLD PATTERNS

In order to permanently eliminate a condition, we must first work to dissolve the mental cause. But most often, since we do not know what the cause is, we find it difficult to know where to begin. So, if you are saying, "If I only knew what is causing this pain," I hope that this booklet will provide both a clue to find the causes and a helpful guide for building new thought patterns which will produce health in mind and body.

I have learned that for every condition in our lives, there is a NEED FOR IT. Otherwise, we would not have it. The symptom is only an outer effect. We must go within to dissolve the mental cause. This is why Willpower and Discipline do not work. They are only battling the outer effect. It is like cutting down the weed instead of getting the root out. So before you begin the New Thought Pattern affirmations, work on the WILLINGNESS TO RELEASE THE NEED for the cigarettes, or the headache, or the excess weight, or whatever. When the need is gone, the outer effect must die. No plant can live if the root is cut away.

The mental thought patterns that cause the most dis-ease in the body are CRITICISM, ANGER, RESENTMENT and GUILT. For instance, criticism indulged in long enough will often lead to diseases such as arthritis. Anger turns into things that boil and burn and infect the body. Resentment long held festers and eats away at the self and ultimately can lead to tumors and cancer. Guilt always seeks punishment and leads to pain. It is so much easier to release these negative thinking patterns from our minds when we are healthy than to try to dig them out when we are in a state of panic and under the threat of the surgeon's knife.

The following list of mental equivalents has been compiled from many years of study, my own work with clients, and my lectures and workshops. It is helpful as a quick-reference guide to the probable mental patterns behind the dis-ease in your body. I offer these with love and a desire to share this simple method of helping to *Heal Your Body*.

HEALING AFFIRMATIONS

PROBLEM	PROBABLE CAUSE	NEW THOUGHT PATTERN
Abdominal Cramps	Fear. Stopping the process.	I trust the process of life. I am safe.
Abscess	Fermenting thoughts over hurts, slights and revenge.	I allow my thoughts to be free. The past is over. I am at peace.
Accidents	Inability to speak up for the self. Rebellion against authority. Belief in violence.	I release the pattern in me that created this. I am at peace. I am worthwhile.
Aches	Longing for love. Longing to be held.	I love and approve of myself. I am loving and lovable.
Acne	Not accepting the self. Dislike of the self.	I am a Divine expression of life. I love and accept myself where I am right now.
Addictions	Running from the self. Fear. Not knowing how to love the self.	I now discover how wonderful I am. I choose to love and enjoy myself.

Addison's Disease See: Adrenal Problems	Severe emotional malnutrition. Anger at the self.	*I lovingly take care of my body, my mind and my emotions.*
Adenoids	Family friction, arguments. Child feeling unwelcome, in the way.	*This child is wanted and welcomed and deeply loved.*
Adrenal Problems See: Addison's Disease, Cushing's Disease	Defeatism. No longer caring for the self. Anxiety.	*I love and approve of myself. It is safe for me to care for myself.*
Aging Problems	Social beliefs. Old thinking. Fear of being one's self. Rejection of the now.	*I love and accept myself at every age. Each moment in life is perfect.*
AIDS	Feeling defenseless and hopeless. Nobody cares. A strong belief in not being good enough. Denial of the self. Sexual guilt.	*I am part of the Universal design. I am important and I am loved by Life itself. I am powerful and capable. I love and appreciate all of myself.*
Alcoholism	"What's the use?" Feeling of futility, guilt, inadequacy. Self-rejection.	*I live in the now. Each moment is new. I choose to see my self-worth. I love and approve of myself.*

Allergies See: Hay Fever	Who are you allergic to? Denying your own power.	*The world is safe and friendly. I am safe. I am at peace with life.*
Alzheimer's Disease See: Dementia, Senility	Refusal to deal with the world as it is. Hopelessness and helplessness. Anger.	*There is always a new and better way for me to experience life. I forgive and release the past. I move into joy.*
Amenorrhea See: Female Problems, Menstrual Problems	Not wanting to be a woman. Dislike of the self.	*I rejoice in who I am. I am a beautiful expression of life, flowing perfectly at all times.*
Amnesia	Fear. Running from life. Inability to stand up for the self.	*Intelligence, courage and self-worth are always present. It is safe to be alive.*
Amyotrophic Lateral Sclerosis (Lou Gehrig's Disease)	Unwillingness to accept self-worth. Denial of success.	*I know I am worthwhile. It is safe for me to succeed. Life loves me.*
Anemia	"Yes-but" attitude. Lack of joy. Fear of life. Not feeling good enough.	*It is safe for me to experience joy in every area of my life. I love life.*

Ankle(s)	Inflexibility and guilt. Ankles represent the ability to receive pleasure.	I deserve to rejoice in life. I accept all the pleasure life has to offer.
Anorectal Bleeding (Hematochezia)	Anger and frustration.	I trust the process of life. Only right and good action is taking place in my life.
Anorexia See: Appetite, Loss of	Denying the self life. Extreme fear, self-hatred and rejection.	It is safe to be me. I am wonderful just as I am. I choose to live. I choose joy and self-acceptance.
Anus See: Hemorrhoids	Releasing point. Dumping ground.	I easily and comfortably release that which I no longer need in life.
– Abscess	Anger in relation to what you don't want to release.	It is safe to let go. Only that which I no longer need leaves my body.
– Bleeding See: Anorectal Bleeding		
– Fistula	Incomplete releasing of trash. Holding on to garbage of the past.	It is with love that I totally release the past. I am free. I am love.
– Itching (Pruritis Ani)	Guilt over the past. Remorse.	I lovingly forgive myself. I am free.

13

– Pain	Guilt. Desire for punishment. Not feeling good enough.	*The past is over. I choose to love and approve of myself in the now.*
Anxiety	Not trusting the flow and the process of life.	*I love and approve of myself and I trust the process of life. I am safe.*
Apathy	Resistance to feeling. Deadening of the self. Fear.	*It is safe to feel. I open myself to life. I am willing to experience life.*
Appendicitis	Fear. Fear of life. Blocking the flow of good.	*I am safe. I relax and let life flow joyously.*
Appetite		
– Excessive	Fear. Needing protection. Judging the emotions.	*I am safe. It is safe to feel. My feelings are normal and acceptable.*
– Loss of See: Anorexia	Fear. Protecting the self. Not trusting life.	*I love and approve of myself. I am safe. Life is safe and joyous.*
Arm(s)	Represents the capacity and ability to hold the experiences of life.	*I lovingly hold and embrace my experiences with ease and with joy.*
Arteries	Carry the joy of life.	*I am filled with joy. It flows through me with every beat of my heart.*

Arteriosclerosis	Resistance, tension. Hardened narrow-mindedness. Refusing to see good.	*I am completely open to life and to joy. I choose to see with love.*
Arthritic Fingers	A desire to punish. Blame. Feeling victimized.	*I see with love and understanding. I hold all my experiences up to the light of love.*
Arthritis See: Joints	Feeling unloved. Criticism, resentment.	*I am love. I now choose to love and approve of myself. I see others with love.*
Asphyxiating Attacks See: Breathing Problems, Hyperventilation	Fear. Not trusting the process of life. Getting stuck in childhood.	*It is safe to grow up. The world is safe. I am safe.*
Asthma	*Smother* love. Inability to breathe for one's self. Feeling stifled. Suppressed crying.	*It is safe now for me to take charge of my own life. I choose to be free.*
—Babies and Children	Fear of life. Not wanting to be here.	*This child is safe and loved. This child is welcomed and cherished.*

Athlete's Foot	Frustration at not being accepted. Inability to move forward with ease.	*I love and approve of myself. I give myself permission to go ahead. It's safe to move.*
Back	Represents the support of life.	*I know that Life always supports me.*
Back Problems See: Spinal Misalignments: Special Section, Page 74		
— Lower	Fear of money. Lack of financial support.	*I trust the process of life. All I need is always taken care of. I am safe.*
— Middle	Guilt. Stuck in all that *stuff* back there. "Get off my back."	*I release the past. I am free to move forward with love in my heart.*
— Upper	Lack of emotional support. Feeling unloved. Holding back love.	*I love and approve of myself. Life supports and loves me.*
Bad Breath See: Halitosis	Anger and revenge thoughts. Experiences backing up.	*I release the past with love. I choose to voice only love.*
Balance, Loss of	Scattered thinking. Not centered.	*I center myself in safety and accept the perfection of my life. All is well.*

16

Baldness	Fear. Tension. Trying to control everything. Not trusting the process of life.	*I am safe. I love and approve of myself. I trust life.*
Bedwetting (Enuresis)	Fear of parent, usually the father.	*This child is seen with love, with compassion and with understanding. All is well.*
Belching	Fear. Gulping life too quickly.	*There is time and space for everything I need to do. I am at peace.*
Bell's Palsy See: Palsy, Paralysis	Extreme control over anger. Unwillingness to express feelings.	*It is safe for me to express my feelings. I forgive myself.*
Birth	Represents the entering of this segment of the movie of life.	*This baby now begins a joyous and wonderful new life. All is well.*
—Defects	Karmic. You selected to come that way. We choose our parents and our children. Unfinished business.	*Every experience is perfect for our growth process. I am at peace with where I am.*
Bites	Fear. Open to every slight.	*I forgive myself and I love myself now and forever more.*
—Animal	Anger turned inward. A need for punishment.	*I am free.*

– Bug	Guilt over small things.	I am free of all irritations. All is well.
Blackheads	Small outbursts of anger.	I calm my thoughts and I am serene.
Bladder Problems (Cystitis)	Anxiety. Holding on to old ideas. Fear of letting go. Being *pissed off*.	I comfortably and easily release the old and welcome the new in my life. I am safe.
Bleeding	Joy running out. Anger. But where?	I am the joy of Life expressing and receiving in perfect rhythm.
Bleeding Gums	Lack of joy in the decision made in life.	I trust that right action is always taking place in my life. I am at peace.
Blisters	Resistance. Lack of emotional protection.	I gently flow with life and each new experience. All is well.
Blood	Represents joy in the body, flowing freely.	I am the joy of Life expressing and receiving.

Blood Pressure

— High Hypertension	Longstanding emotional problem not solved.	*I joyously release the past. I am at peace.*
— Low	Lack of love as a child. Defeatism. "What's the use? It won't work anyway."	*I now choose to live in the ever-joyous NOW. My life is a joy.*
Blood Problems See: Leukemia	Lack of joy. Lack of circulation of ideas.	*Joyous new ideas are circulating freely within me.*
— Anemic See: Anemia		
— Clotting	Closing down the flow of joy.	*I awaken new life within me. I flow.*
Body Odor	Fear. Dislike of the self. Fear of others.	*I love and approve of myself. I am safe.*
Boils (Furuncle) See: Carbuncle	Anger. Boiling over. Seething.	*I express love and joy and I am at peace.*
Bone(s) See: Skeleton	Represent the structure of the Universe.	*I am well structured and balanced.*

19

Bone Marrow	Represents deepest beliefs about the self. How you support and care for yourself.	*Divine Spirit is the structure of my life. I am safe and loved and totally supported.*
Bone Problems		
— Breaks/Fractures	Rebelling against authority.	*In my world, I am my own authority; for I am the only one who thinks in my mind.*
— Deformity See: Osteomyelitis, Osteoporosis	Mental pressures and tightness. Muscles can't stretch. Loss of mental mobility.	*I breathe in life fully. I relax and trust the flow and the process of life.*
Bowels	Represent the release of waste.	*Letting go is easy.*
— Problems	Fear of letting go of the old and no longer needed.	*I freely and easily release the old and joyously welcome the new.*
Brain	Represents the computer, the switchboard.	*I am the loving operator of my mind.*
— Tumor	Incorrect computerized beliefs. Stubborn. Refusing to change old patterns.	*It is easy for me to reprogram the computer of my mind. All of life is change and my mind is ever new.*

Breast(s)	Represents mothering and nurturing and nourishment.	*I take in and give out nourishment in perfect balance.*
Breast Problems	A refusal to nourish the self. Putting everyone else first. Overmothering. Overprotection. Overbearing attitudes.	*I am important. I count. I now care for and nourish myself with love and with joy. I allow others the freedom to be who they are. We are all safe and free.*
— Cysts, Lumps, Soreness (Mastitis)		
Breath	Represents the ability to take in life.	*I love life. It is safe to live.*
Breathing Problems See: Asphyxiating Attacks, Hyperventilation	Fear or refusal to take in life fully. Not feeling the right to take up space or even exist.	*It is my birthright to live life fully and freely. I am worth loving. I now choose to live life fully.*
Bright's Disease See: Nephritis	Feeling like a kid who can't do it right and is not good enough. A failure. Loss.	*I love and approve of myself. I care for me. I am totally adequate at all times.*
Bronchitis See: Respiratory Ailments	Inflamed family environment. Arguments and yelling. Sometimes silent.	*I declare peace and harmony within me and around me. All is well.*
Bruises (Ecchymoses)	The little bumps in life. Self-punishment.	*I love and cherish myself. I am kind and gentle with me. All is well.*

21

Bulimia	Hopeless terror. A frantic stuffing and purging of self-hatred.	*I am loved and nourished and supported by Life itself. It is safe for me to be alive.*
Bunions	Lack of joy in meeting the experiences of life.	*I joyously run forward to greet life's wonderful experiences.*
Burns	Anger. Burning up. Incensed.	*I create only peace and harmony within myself and in my environment. I deserve to feel good.*
Bursitis	Repressed anger. Wanting to hit someone.	*Love relaxes and releases all unlike itself.*
Buttocks	Represent power. Loose Buttocks, loss of power.	*I use my power wisely. I am strong. I am safe. All is well.*
Callouses	Hardened concepts and ideas. Fear solidified.	*It is safe to see and experience new ideas and new ways. I am open and receptive to good.*
Cancer	Deep hurt. Longstanding resentment. Deep secret or grief eating away at the self. Carrying hatreds. "What's the use?"	*I lovingly forgive and release all of the past. I choose to fill my world with joy. I love and approve of myself.*

22

Candida (Candidiasis) See: Thrush, Yeast Infections	Feeling very scattered. Lots of frustration and anger. Demanding and untrusting in relationships. Great takers.	*I give myself permission to be all that I can be and I deserve the very best in life. I love and appreciate myself and others.*
Canker Sores	Festering words held back by the lips. Blame.	*I create only joyful experiences in my loving world.*
Car Sickness See: Motion Sickness	Fear. Bondage. Feeling of being trapped.	*I move with ease through time and space. Only love surrounds me.*
Carbuncle See: Boils	Poisonous anger about personal injustices.	*I release the past and allow time to heal every area of my life.*
Carpal-Tunnel Syndrome See: Wrist	Anger and frustration at life's seeming injustices.	*I now choose to create a life that is joyous and abundant. I am at ease.*
Cataracts	Inability to see ahead with joy. Dark future.	*Life is eternal and filled with joy. I look forward to every moment.*
Cellulite	Stored anger and self-punishment.	*I forgive others. I forgive myself. I am free to love and enjoy life.*
Cerebral Palsy See: Palsy	A need to unite the family in an action of love.	*I contribute to a united, loving and peaceful family life. All is well.*

Cerebrovascular Accident See: Stroke		
Childhood Diseases	Belief in calendars and social concepts and false laws. Childish behavior in the adults around them.	*This child is Divinely protected and surrounded by love. We claim mental immunity.*
Chills	Mental contraction, pulling away and in. Desire to retreat. "Leave me alone."	*I am safe and secure at all times. Love surrounds me and protects me. All is well.*
Cholelithiasis See: Gallstones		
Cholesterol (Atherosclerosis)	Clogging the channels of joy. Fear of accepting joy.	*I choose to love life. My channels of joy are wide open. It is safe to receive.*
Chronic Diseases	A refusal to change. Fear of the future. Not feeling safe.	*I am willing to change and to grow. I now create a safe, new future.*
Circulation	Represents the ability to feel and express the emotions in positive ways.	*I am free to circulate love and joy in every part of my world. I love life.*

24

Cold Sores (Fever Blisters) See: Herpes Simplex	Festering angry words and fear of expressing them.	*I only create peaceful experiences because I love myself. All is well.*
Colds (Upper-Respiratory Illness) See: Respiratory Ailments	Too much going on at once. Mental confusion, disorder. Small hurts. "I get three colds every winter," type of belief.	*I allow my mind to relax and be at peace. Clarity and harmony are within me and around me. All is well.*
Colic	Mental irritation, impatience, annoyance in the surroundings.	*This child responds only to love and to loving thoughts. All is peaceful.*
Colitis See: Colon, Intestines, Mucus Colon, Spastic Colitis	Insecurity. Represents the ease of letting go of that which is over.	*I am part of the perfect rhythm and flow of life. All is in Divine right order.*
Coma	Fear. Escaping something or someone.	*We surround you with safety and love. We create a space for you to heal. You are loved.*
Comedones	Small outbursts of anger.	*I calm my thoughts and I am serene.*

Congestion
See: Bronchitis,
Colds, Influenza

Conjunctivitis
See: Pink Eye

Constipation   Refusing to release old ideas. Stuck in the past. Sometimes stinginess.   *As I release the past, the new and fresh and vital enter. I allow life to flow through me.*

Corns   Hardened areas of thought – stubborn holding on to the pain of the past.   *I move forward free from the past. I am safe, I am free.*

Coronary Thrombosis
See: Heart Attack   Feeling alone and scared. "I'm not good enough. I don't do enough. I'll never make it."   *I am one with all of life. The Universe totally supports me. All is well.*

Coughs
See: Respiratory
Ailments   A desire to bark at the world. "See me! Listen to me!"   *I am noticed and appreciated in the most positive ways. I am loved.*

I see with eyes of love. There is a harmonious solution and I accept it now. (Conjunctivitis)

Anger and frustration at what you are looking at in life. (Conjunctivitis)

26

Cramps	Tension. Fear. Gripping, holding on.	*I relax and allow my mind to be peaceful.*
Croup See: Bronchitis		
Crying	Tears are the river of life, shed in joy as well as in sadness and fear.	*I am peaceful with all of my emotions. I love and approve of myself.*
Cushing's Disease See: Adrenal Problems	Mental imbalance. Overproduction of crushing ideas. A feeling of being overpowered.	*I lovingly balance my mind and my body. I now choose thoughts that make me feel good.*
Cuts See: Injuries, Wounds	Punishment for not following your own rules.	*I create a life filled with rewards.*
Cyst(s)	Running the old painful movie. Nursing hurts. A false growth.	*The movies of my mind are beautiful because I choose to make them so. I love me.*
Cystic Fibrosis	A thick belief that life won't work for you. "Poor me."	*Life loves me, and I love life. I now choose to take in life fully and freely.*

27

Cystitis
See: Bladder Problems

Deafness	Rejection, stubbornness, isolation. What don't you want to hear? "Don't bother me."	*I listen to the Divine and rejoice at all that I am able to hear. I am one with all.*
Death	Represents leaving the movie of life.	*I joyfully move on to new levels of experience. All is well.*
Dementia See: Alzheimer's Disease, Senility	A refusal to deal with the world as it is. Hopelessness and anger.	*I am in my perfect place and I am safe at all times.*
Depression	Anger you feel you do not have a right to have. Hopelessness.	*I now go beyond other people's fears and limitations. I create my life.*
Diabetes **(Hyperglycemia, Mellitus)**	Longing for what might have been. A great need to control. Deep sorrow. No sweetness left.	*This moment is filled with joy. I now choose to experience the sweetness of today.*
Diarrhea	Fear. Rejection. Running off.	*My intake, assimilation and elimination are in perfect order. I am at peace with life.*

Dizziness (Vertigo)	Flighty, scattered thinking. A refusal to look.
	I am deeply centered and peaceful in life. It is safe for me to be alive and joyous.
Dry Eye	Angry eyes. Refusing to see with love. Would rather die than forgive. Being spiteful.
	I willingly forgive. I breathe life into my vision and see with compassion and understanding.
Dysentery	Fear and intense anger.
	I create peacefulness in my mind and my body reflects this.
— Amoebic	Believing *they* are out to get you.
	I am the power and authority in my world. I am at peace.
— Bacillary	Oppression and hopelessness.
	I am filled with life and energy and the joy of living.
Dysmenorrhea See: Female Problems, Menstrual Problems	Anger at the self. Hatred of the body or of women.
	I love my body. I love myself. I love all my cycles. All is well.
Ear(s)	Represents the capacity to hear.
	I hear with love.
Earache (Otitis: External/Ear Canal Media/Inner Ear)	Anger. Not wanting to hear. Too much turmoil. Parents arguing.
	Harmony surrounds me. I listen with love to the pleasant and the good. I am a center for love.

Ecchymoses
See: Bruises

Exzema

Breath-taking antagonism. Mental eruptions.

Harmony and peace, love and joy surround me and indwell me. I am safe and secure.

Edema
See: Holding Fluids, Swelling

What or who won't you let go of?

I willingly release the past. It is safe for me to let go. I am free now.

Elbow
See: Joints

Represents changing directions and accepting new experiences.

I easily flow with new experiences, new directions and new changes.

Emphysema

Fear of taking in life. Not worthy of living.

It is my birthright to live fully and freely. I love life. I love me.

Endometriosis

Insecurity, disappointment and frustration. Replacing self-love with sugar. Blamers.

I am both powerful and desirable. It's wonderful to be a woman. I love myself and I am fulfilled.

Enuresis
See: Bedwetting

Epilepsy

Sense of persecution. Rejection of life. A feeling of great struggle. Self-violence.

I choose to see life as eternal and joyous. I am eternal and joyous and at peace.

Epstein-Barr Virus — Pushing beyond one's limits. Fear of not being good enough. Draining all inner support. Stress virus. — I relax and recognize my self-worth. I am good enough. Life is easy and joyful.

Exotropia
See: Eye Problems

Eye(s) — Represents the capacity to see clearly—past, present and future. — I see with love and joy.

Eye problems
See: Sty

—**Astigmatism** — Not liking what you see in your own life. — I now create a life I love to look at.

—**Cataracts** — "I" trouble. Fear of really seeing the self. — I am now willing to see my own beauty and magnificence.

—**Children** — Inability to see ahead with joy. Dark future. — Life is eternal and filled with joy.

—**Crossed**
See: Keratitis — Not wanting to see what is going on in the family. — Harmony and joy and beauty and safety now surround this child.

— Not wanting to see what's out there. Crossed purposes. — It is safe for me to see. I am at peace.

—**Farsighted**
(Hyperopia) — Fear of the present. — I am safe in the here and now. I see that clearly.

31

—Glaucoma	Stony unforgiveness. Pressure from longstanding hurts. Overwhelmed by it all.	I see with love and tenderness.
—Nearsighted
See: Myopia	Fear of the future.	I accept Divine guidance and am always safe.
—Wall Eyed
(Exotropia)	Fear of looking at the present, right here.	I love and approve of myself right now.
Face	Represents what we show the world.	It is safe to be me. I express who I am.
Fainting (Vasovagal Attack)	Fear. Can't cope. Blacking out.	I have the power and strength and knowledge to handle everything in my life.
Fat
See: Overweight	Oversensitivity. Often represents fear and shows a need for protection. Fear may be a cover for hidden anger and a resistance to forgive.	I am protected by Divine Love. I am always safe and secure. I am willing to grow up and take responsibility for my life. I forgive others and I now create my own life the way I want it. I am safe.

— Arms	Anger at being denied love.	*It is safe for me to create all the love I want.*
— Belly	Anger at being denied nourishment.	*I nourish myself with spiritual food and I am satisfied and free.*
— Hips	Lumps of stubborn anger at the parents.	*I am willing to forgive the past. It is safe for me to go beyond my parents' limitations.*
— Thighs	Packed childhood anger. Often rage at the father.	*I see my father as a loveless child and I forgive easily. We are both free.*
Fatigue	Resistance, boredom. Lack of love for what one does.	*I am enthusiastic about life and filled with energy and enthusiasm.*
Feet	Represent our understanding — of ourselves, of life, of others.	*My understanding is clear, and I am willing to change with the times. I am safe.*

Female Problems
See: Amenorrhea,
Dysmenorrhea,
Fibroid Tumors,
Leukorrhea,
Menstrual Problems,
Vaginitis

Denial of the self. Rejecting femininity. Rejection of the feminine principle.

I rejoice in my femaleness. I love being a woman. I love my body.

Fever

Anger. Burning up.

I am the cool, calm expression of peace and love.

Fever Blisters
See: Cold Sores,
Herpes Simplex

Fibroid Tumors & Cysts
See: Female Problems

Nursing a hurt from a partner. A blow to the feminine ego.

I release the pattern in me that attracted this experience. I create only good in my life.

Fingers

Represent the details of life.

I am peaceful with the details of life.

—Thumb

Represents intellect and worry.

My mind is at peace.

—Index Finger

Represents ego and fear.

I am secure.

34

– Middle Finger	Represents anger and sexuality.	I am comfortable with my sexuality.
– Ring Finger	Represents unions and grief.	I am peacefully loving.
– Little Finger	Represents the family and pretending.	I am myself with the family of Life.
Fistula	Fear. A blockage in the letting go process.	I am safe. I trust fully in the process of life. Life is for me.

Flatulence
See: Gas Pains

Flu
See: Influenza

| **Food Poisoning** | Allowing others to take control. Feeling defenseless. | I have the strength, power, and skill to digest whatever comes my way. |
| **Foot Problems** | Fear of the future and of not stepping forward in life. | I move forward in life with joy and with ease. |

Fractures
See: Bone Problems

35

Frigidity	Fear. Denial of pleasure. A belief that sex is bad. Insensitive partners. Fear of father.	*It is safe for me to enjoy my own body. I rejoice in being a woman.*
Fungus	Stagnating beliefs. Refusing to release the past. Letting the past rule today.	*I live in the present moment, joyous and free.*
Furuncle See: Boils		
Gallstones (Cholelithiasis)	Bitterness. Hard thoughts. Condemning. Pride.	*There is joyous release of the past. Life is sweet, and so am I.*
Gangrene	Mental morbidity. Drowning of joy with poisonous thoughts.	*I now choose harmonious thoughts and let the joy flow freely through me.*
Gas Pains (Flatulence)	Gripping. Fear. Undigested ideas.	*I relax and let life flow through me with ease.*
Gastritis See: Stomach Problems	Prolonged uncertainty. A feeling of doom.	*I love and approve of myself. I am safe.*
Genitals	Represent the masculine and feminine principles.	*It is safe to be who I am.*

—Problems	Worry about not being good enough.	*I rejoice in my own expression of life. I am perfect just as I am. I love and approve of myself.*
Gland(s)	Represent holding stations. Self-starting activity.	*I am the creative power in my world.*
Glandular Fever See: Mononucleosis		
Glandular Problems	Poor distribution of get-up-and-go ideas. Holding yourself back.	*I have all the Divine ideas and activity I need. I move foward right now.*
Globus Hystericus See: Lump in Throat		
Goiter See: Thyroid	Hatred for being inflicted upon. Victim. Feeling thwarted in life. Unfulfilled.	*I am the power and authority in my life. I am free to be me.*
Gonorrhea See: Venereal Disease	A need for punishment for being a *bad* person.	*I love my body. I love my sexuality. I love me.*
Gout	The need to dominate. Impatience, anger.	*I am safe and secure. I am at peace with myself and with others.*

Gray Hair	Stress. A belief in pressure and strain.	*I am at peace and comfortable in every area of my life. I am strong and capable.*
Growths	Nursing those old hurts. Building resentments.	*I easily forgive. I love myself and will reward myself with thoughts of praise.*
Gum Problems	Inability to back up decisions. Wishy-washy about life.	*I am a decisive person. I follow through and support myself with love.*
Halitosis See: Bad Breath	Rotten attitudes, vile gossip, foul thinking.	*I speak with gentleness and love. I exhale only the good.*
Hands	Hold and handle. Clutch and grip. Grasping and letting go. Caressing. Pinching. All ways of dealing with experiences.	*I choose to handle all my experiences with love and with joy and with ease.*
Hay Fever See: Allergies	Emotional congestion. Fear of the calendar. A belief in persecution. Guilt.	*I am one with ALL OF LIFE. I am safe at all times.*

Headaches
See: Migraine Headaches

Invalidating the self. Self-criticism. Fear.

I love and approve of myself. I see myself and what I do with eyes of love. I am safe.

Heart
See: Blood

Represents the center of love and security.

My heart beats to the rhythm of love.

—Attack
(M.I./Myocardial Infarction)
See: Coronary Thrombosis

Squeezing all the joy out of the heart in favor of money or position, etc.

I bring joy back to the center of my heart. I express love to all.

—Problems

Longstanding emotional problems. Lack of joy. Hardening of the heart. Belief in strain and stress.

Joy. Joy. Joy. I lovingly allow joy to flow through my mind and body and experience.

Heartburn
See: Peptic Ulcer, Stomach Problems, Ulcers

Fear. Fear. Fear. Clutching fear.

I breathe freely and fully. I am safe. I trust the process of life.

39

Hematochezia
See: Anorectal
Bleeding

Hemorrhoids
See: Anus

Hepatitis
See: Liver Problems

Fear of deadlines. Anger of the past. Afraid to let go. Feeling burdened.

I release all that is unlike love. There is time and space for everything I want to do.

Resistance to change. Fear, anger, hatred. Liver is the seat of anger and rage.

My mind is cleansed and free. I leave the past and move into the new. All is well.

Hernia

Ruptured relationships. Strain, burdens, incorrect creative expression.

My mind is gentle and harmonious. I love and approve of myself. I am free to be me.

Herpes
(Herpes Genitalis)
See: Venereal Disease

Mass belief in sexual guilt and the need for punishment. Public shame. Belief in a punishing God. Rejection of the genitals.

My concept of God supports me. I am normal and natural. I rejoice in my own sexuality and in my own body. I am wonderful.

Herpes Simplex
(Herpes Labialis)
See: Cold Sores

Burning to bitch. Bitter words left unspoken.

I think and speak only words of love. I am at peace with life.

Hip(s)

Carries the body in perfect balance. Major thrust in moving forward.

Hip Hip Hooray — there is joy in every day. I am balanced and free.

40

Hip Problems	Fear of going forward in major decisions. Nothing to move forward to.	*I am in perfect balance. I move forward in life with ease and with joy at every age.*
Hirsutism	Anger that is covered over. The blanket used is usually fear. A desire to blame. There is often an unwillingness to nurture the self.	*I am a loving parent to myself. I am covered with love and approval. It is safe for me to show who I am.*
Hives (Urticaria) See: Rash	Small, hidden fears. Mountains out of molehills.	*I bring peace to every corner of my life.*
Hodgkin's Disease	Blame and a tremendous fear of not being good enough. A frantic race to prove one's self until the blood has no substance left to support itself. The joy of life is forgotten in the race for acceptance.	*I am perfectly happy to be me. I am good enough just as I am. I love and approve of myself. I am joy expressing and receiving.*
Holding Fluids See: Edema, Swelling	What are you afraid of losing?	*I willingly release with joy.*
Huntington's Disease	Resentment at not being able to change others. Hopelessness.	*I release all control to the Universe. I am at peace with myself and with life.*

41

Hyperactivity	Fear. Feeling pressured and frantic	*I am safe. All pressure dissolves. I AM good enough.*
Hyperglycemia See: Diabetes		
Hyperopia See: Eye Problems		
Hypertension See: Blood Pressure		
Hyperthyroidism See: Thyroid	Rage at being left out.	*I am at the center of life and I approve of myself and all that I see.*
Hyperventilation See: Asphyxiating Attacks, Breathing Problems	Fear. Resisting change. Not trusting the process.	*I am safe everywhere in the Universe. I love myself and trust the process of life.*
Hypoglycemia	Overwhelmed by the burdens in life. "What's the use?"	*I now choose to make my life light and easy and joyful.*
Hypothyroidism See: Thyroid	Giving up. Feeling hopelessly stifled.	*I create a new life with new rules that totally support me.*

Ileitis (Crohn's Disease, Regional Enteritis)	Fear. Worry. Not feeling good enough.	*I love and approve of myself. I am doing the best I can. I am wonderful. I am at peace.*
Impotence	Sexual pressure, tension, guilt. Social beliefs. Spite against a previous mate. Fear of mother.	*I now allow the full power of my sexual principle to operate with ease and with joy.*
Incontinence	Emotional overflow. Years of controlling the emotions.	*I am willing to feel. It is safe for me to express my emotions. I love myself.*
Incurable	Cannot be cured by outer means at this point. We must go within to effect the cure. It came from nowhere and will go back to nowhere.	*Miracles happen every day. I go within to dissolve the pattern that created this, and I now accept a Divine healing. And so it is!*
Indigestion	Gut-level fear, dread, anxiety. Griping and grunting.	*I digest and assimilate all new experiences peacefully and joyously.*
Infection See: Viral Infection	Irritation, anger, annoyance.	*I choose to be peaceful and harmonious.*

Inflammation See: "Itis"	Fear. Seeing red. Inflamed thinking.	*My thinking is peaceful, calm and centered.*
Influenza See: Respiratory Ailments	Response to mass negativity and beliefs. Fear. Belief in statistics.	*I am beyond group beliefs or the calendar. I am free from all congestion and influence.*
Ingrown Toenail	Worry and guilt about your right to move forward.	*It is my Divine right to take my own direction in life. I am safe. I am free.*
Injuries See: Cuts, Wounds	Anger at the self. Feeling guilty.	*I now release anger in positive ways. I love and appreciate myself.*
Insanity (Psychiatric Illness)	Fleeing from the family. Escapism, withdrawal. Violent separation from life.	*This mind knows its true identity and is a creative point of Divine Self-Expression.*
Insomnia	Fear. Not trusting the process of life. Guilt.	*I lovingly release the day and slip into peaceful sleep, knowing tomorrow will take care of itself.*
Intestines See: Colon	Assimilation. Absorption. Elimination with ease.	*I easily assimilate and absorb all that I need to know and release the past with joy.*

Itching (Pruritis)	Desires that go against the grain. Unsatisfied. Remorse. Itching to get out or get away.	*I am at peace just where I am. I accept my good, knowing all my needs and desires will be fulfilled.*
"Itis" See: Inflammation	Anger and frustration about conditions you are looking at in your life.	*I am willing to change all patterns of criticism. I love and approve of myself.*
Jaundice See: Liver Problems	Internal and external prejudice. Unbalanced reason.	*I feel tolerance and compassion and love for all people, myself included.*
Jaw Problems (Temporomandibular Joint, TMJ Syndrome)	Anger. Resentment. Desire for revenge.	*I am willing to change the patterns in me that created this condition. I love and approve of myself. I am safe.*
Joints See: Arthritis, Elbow, Knee, Shoulders	Represent changes in direction in life and the ease of these movements.	*I easily flow with change. My life is Divinely guided and I am always going in the best direction.*
Keratitis See: Eye Problems	Extreme anger. A desire to hit those or what you see.	*I allow the love from my own heart to heal all that I see. I choose peace. All is well in my world.*

45

Kidney Problems	Criticism, disappointment, failure. Shame. Reacting like a little kid.	*Divine right action is always taking place in my life. Only good comes from each experience. It is safe to grow up.*
Kidney Stones	Lumps of undissolved anger.	*I dissolve all past problems with ease.*
Knee See: Joints	Represents pride and ego.	*I am flexible and flowing.*
Knee Problems	Stubborn ego and pride. Inability to bend. Fear. Inflexibility. Won't give in.	*Forgiveness. Understanding. Compassion. I bend and flow with ease, and all is well.*
Laryngitis	So mad you can't speak. Fear of speaking up. Resentment of authority.	*I am free to ask for what I want. It is safe to express myself. I am at peace.*
Left Side of Body	Represents receptivity, taking in, feminine energy, women, the mother.	*My feminine energy is beautifully balanced.*
Leg(s)	Carry us forward in life.	*Life is for me.*

46

Leg Problems – Lower	Fear of the future. Not wanting to move.	I move forward with confidence and joy, knowing that all is well in my future.
Leprosy	Inability to handle life at all. A long-held belief in not being good enough or clean enough.	I rise above all limitations. I am Divinely guided and inspired. Love heals all life.
Leukemia See: Blood Problems	Brutally killing inspiration. "What's the use?"	I move beyond past limitations into the freedom of the now. It is safe to be me.
Leukorrhea See: Female Problems, Vaginitis	A belief that women are powerless over the opposite sex. Anger at a mate.	I create all my experiences. I am the power. I rejoice in my femaleness. I am free.
Liver	Seat of anger and primitive emotions.	Love and peace and joy are what I know.
Liver Problems See: Hepatitis, Jaundice	Chronic complaining. Justifying fault-finding to deceive yourself. Feeling bad.	I choose to live through the open space in my heart. I look for love and find it everywhere.
Lockjaw See: Tetanus	Anger. A desire to control. A refusal to express feelings.	I trust the process of life. I easily ask for what I want. Life supports me.

Lou Gehrig's Disease See: Amyotrophic Lateral Sclerosis		
Lump in Throat (Globus Hystericus)	Fear. Not trusting the process of life.	*I am safe. I trust that Life is here for me. I express myself freely and joyously.*
Lung	The ability to take in life.	*I take in life in perfect balance.*
— Problems See: Pneumonia	Depression. Grief. Fear of taking in life. Not feeling worthy of living life fully.	*I have the capacity to take in the fullness of life. I lovingly live life to the fullest.*
Lupus (Erythematosus)	A giving up. Better to die than stand up for one's self. Anger and punishment.	*I speak up for myself freely and easily. I claim my own power. I love and approve of myself. I am free and safe.*
Lymph Problems	A warning that the mind needs to be recentered on the essentials of life. Love and Joy.	*I am now totally centered in the love and joy of being alive. I flow with life. Peace of mind is mine.*
Malaria	Out of balance with nature and with life.	*I am united and balanced with all of life. I am safe.*

48

Mastitis
See: Breast Problems

Mastoiditis

Anger and frustration. A desire not to hear what is going on. Usually in children. Fear infecting the understanding.

Divine peace and harmony surround and indwell me. I am an oasis of peace and love and joy. All is well in my world.

Mellitus
See: Diabetes

Menopause Problems

Fear of no longer being wanted. Fear of aging. Self-rejection. Not feeling good enough.

I am balanced and peaceful in all changes of cycles, and I bless my body with love.

Menstrual Problems
See: Amenorrhea, Dysmenorrhea, Female Problems

Rejection of one's femininity. Guilt, fear. Belief that the genitals are sinful or dirty.

I accept my full power as a woman and accept all my bodily processes as normal and natural. I love and approve of myself.

Migraine Headaches
See: Headaches

Dislike of being driven. Resisting the flow of life. Sexual fears. (Can usually be relieved by masturbation.)

I relax into the flow of life and let life provide all that I need easily and comfortably. Life is for me.

Miscarriage (Abortion, Spontaneous)	Fear. Fear of the future. "Not now — later." Inappropriate timing.	*Divine right action is always taking place in my life. I love and approve of myself. All is well.*
Mono., Mononucleosis (Pfeiffer's Disease, Glandular Fever)	Anger at not receiving love and appreciation. No longer caring for the self.	*I love and appreciate and take care of myself. I am enough.*
Motion Sickness See: Car Sickness, Seasickness	Fear. Fear of not being in control.	*I am always in control of my thoughts. I am safe. I love and approve of myself.*
Mouth	Represents taking in of new ideas and nourishment.	*I nourish myself with love.*
—Problems	Set opinions. Closed mind. Incapacity to take in new ideas.	*I welcome new ideas and new concepts and prepare them for digestion and assimilation.*
Mucus Colon See: Colitis, Colon, Intestines, Spastic Colitis	Layered deposits of old, confused thoughts clogging the channel of elimination. Wallowing in the gummed mire of the past.	*I release and dissolve the past. I am a clear thinker. I live in the now in peace and joy.*
Multiple Sclerosis	Mental hardness, hard-heartedness, iron will, inflexibility. Fear.	*By choosing loving, joyous thoughts, I create a loving, joyous world. I am safe and free.*

Muscles	Resistance to new experiences. Muscles represent our ability to move in life.	*I experience life as a joyous dance.*
Muscular Dystrophy	"It's not worth growing up."	*I go beyond my parents' limitations. I am free to be the best me I can.*
Myalgic Encephalomyelitis See: Epstein-Barr Virus		
Myocardial Infarction See: Heart Attack		
Myopia See: Eye Problems	Fear of the future. Not trusting what is ahead.	*I trust the process of life. I am safe.*
Nail(s)	Represent protection.	*I reach out safely.*
Nail Biting	Frustration. Eating away at the self. Spite of a parent.	*It is safe for me to grow up. I now handle my own life with joy and with ease.*

Narcolepsy	Can't cope. Extreme fear. Wanting to get away from it all. Not wanting to be here.	*I rely on Divine wisdom and guidance to protect me at all times. I am safe.*
Nausea	Fear. Rejecting an idea or experience.	*I am safe. I trust the process of life to bring only good to me.*
Nearsightedness See: Eye Problems, Myopia		
Neck (Cervical Spine)	Represents flexibility. The ability to see what's back there.	*I am peaceful with life.*
Neck Problems See: Spinal Misalignments: Special Section, Page74, Stiff Neck	Refusing to see other sides of a question. Stubbornness, inflexibility.	*It is with flexibility and ease that I see all sides of an issue. There are endless ways of doing things and seeing things. I am safe.*
Nephritis See: Bright's Disease	Overreaction to disappointment and failure.	*Only right action is taking place in my life. I release the old and welcome the new. All is well.*

Nerves	Represent communication. Receptive reporters.	I communicate with ease and with joy.
Nervous Breakdown	Self-centeredness. Jamming the channels of communication.	I open my heart and create only loving communication. I am safe. I am well.
Nervousness	Fear, anxiety, struggle, rushing. Not trusting the process of life.	I am on an endless journey through eternity and there is plenty of time. I communicate with my heart. All is well.
Neuralgia	Punishment for guilt. Anguish over communication.	I forgive myself. I love and approve of myself. I communicate with love.
Nodules	Resentment and frustration and hurt ego over career.	I release the pattern of delay within me, and I now allow success to be mine.
Nose	Represents self-recognition.	I recognize my own intuitive ability.
— Bleeds	A need for recognition. Feeling unrecognized and unnoticed. Crying for love.	I love and approve of myself. I recognize my own true worth. I am wonderful.
— Runny	Asking for help. Inner crying.	I love and comfort myself in ways that are pleasing to me.

— Stuffy	Not recognizing the self-worth.	*I love and appreciate myself.*
Numbness (Paresthesia)	Withholding love and consideration. Going dead mentally.	*I share my feelings and my love. I respond to love in everyone.*
Osteomyelitis See: Bone Problems	Anger and frustration at the very structure of life. Feeling unsupported.	*I am peaceful with and trust the process of life. I am safe and secure.*
Osteoporosis See: Bone Problems	Feeling there is no support left in life.	*I stand up for myself and Life supports me in unexpected, loving ways.*
Ovaries	Represent points of creation. Creativity.	*I am balanced in my creative flow.*
Overweight See: Fat	Fear, need for protection. Running away from feelings. Insecurity, self-rejection. Seeking fulfillment.	*I am at peace with my own feelings. I am safe where I am. I create my own security. I love and approve of myself.*
Paget's Disease	Feeling there is no longer any foundation to build on. "Nobody cares."	*I know I am supported by Life in grand and glorious ways. Life loves me and cares for me.*

54

Pain	Guilt. Guilt always seeks punishment.	*I lovingly release the past. They are free and I am free. All is well in my heart now.*
Palsy See: Bell's, Paralysis, Parkinson's Disease	Paralysing thoughts. Getting stuck.	*I am a free thinker and I have wonderful experiences with ease and with joy.*
Pancreas	Represents the sweetness of life.	*My life is sweet.*
Pancreatitis	Rejection. Anger and frustration because life seems to have lost its sweetness.	*I love and approve of myself, and I alone create sweetness and joy in my life.*
Paralysis See: Palsy	Fear. Terror. Escaping a situation or person. Resistance.	*I am one with all of life. I am totally adequate for all situations.*
Parasites	Giving power to others, letting them take over.	*I lovingly take back my power and eliminate all interference.*
Paresthesia See: Numbness		
Parkinson's Disease See: Palsy	Fear and an intense desire to control everything and everyone.	*I relax knowing that I am safe. Life is for me and I trust the process of life.*

55

Peptic Ulcer
See: Heartburn,
Stomach Problems,
Ulcers

Fear. A belief that you are not good enough. Anxious to please.

I love and approve of myself. I am at peace with myself. I am wonderful.

Periodontitis
See: Pyorrhea

Petit Mal
See: Epilepsy

Pfeiffer's Disease
See: Mononucleosis

Phlebitis

Anger and frustration. Blaming others for the limitation and lack of joy in life.

Joy now flows freely within me, and I am at peace with life.

Piles
See: Hemorrhoids

Pimples
See: Blackheads,
Whiteheads

Small outbursts of anger.

I calm my thoughts and I am serene.

Pink Eye See: Conjunctivitis	Anger and frustration. Not wanting to see.	*I release the need to be right. I am at peace. I love and approve of myself.*
Pituitary Gland	Represents the control center.	*My mind and body are in perfect balance. I control my thoughts.*
Plantar Wart	Anger at the very basis of your understanding. Spreading frustration about the future.	*I move forward with confidence and ease. I trust and flow with the process of life.*
Pneumonia See: Lung Problems	Desperate. Tired of life. Emotional wounds that are not allowed to heal.	*I freely take in Divine ideas that are filled with the breath and the intelligence of Life. This is a new moment.*
Poison Ivy	Feeling defenseless and open to attack.	*I am powerful, safe and secure. All is well.*
Poison Oak See: Poison Ivy		
Polio	Paralysing jealousy. A desire to stop someone.	*There is enough for everyone. I create my good and my freedom with loving thoughts.*

Post-Nasal Drip	Inner crying. Childish tears. Victim.	*I acknowledge and accept that I am the creative power in my world. I now choose to enjoy my life.*
Premenstrual Syndrome (PMS)	Allowing confusion to reign. Giving power to outside influences. Rejection of the feminine processes.	*I now take charge of my mind and my life. I am a powerful, dynamic woman! Every part of my body functions perfectly. I love me.*
Prostate	Represents the masculine principle.	*I accept and rejoice in my masculinity.*
Prostate Problems	Mental fears weaken the masculinity. Giving up. Sexual pressure and guilt. Belief in aging.	*I love and approve of myself. I accept my own power. I am forever young in spirit.*
Pruritis See: Itching		
Pruritis Ani See: Anus		
Psoriasis See: Skin Problems	Fear of being hurt. Deadening the senses of the self. Refusing to accept responsibility for our own feelings.	*I am alive to the joys of living. I deserve and accept the very best in life. I love and approve of myself.*

Psychiatric Illness
See: Insanity

Pubic Bone

Represents genital protection.

My sexuality is safe.

Pyelonephritis
See: Urinary Infections

Pyorrhea (Periodontitis)

Anger at the inability to make decisions. Wishy-washy people.

I approve of myself, and my decisions are always perfect for me.

Quinsy (Peritonsillar Abscess)
See: Sore Throat, Tonsillitis

A strong belief that you cannot speak up for yourself and ask for your needs.

It is my birthright to have my needs met. I now ask for what I want with love and with ease.

Rabies

Anger. A belief that violence is the answer.

I am surrounded and indwelled with peace.

Rash
See: Hives

Irritation over delays. Babyish way to get attention.

I love and approve of myself. I am at peace with the process of life.

Rectum
See: Anus

Respiratory Ailments See: Bronchitis, Colds, Coughs, Influenza	Fear of taking in life fully.	*I am safe. I love my life.*
Rheumatism	Feeling victimized. Lack of love. Chronic bitterness. Resentment.	*I create my own experiences. As I love and approve of myself and others, my experiences get better and better.*
Rheumatoid Arthritis	Deep criticism of authority. Feeling very put upon.	*I am my own authority. I love and approve of myself. Life is good.*
Rickets	Emotional malnutrition. Lack of love and security.	*I am secure and am nourished by the love of the Universe itself.*
Right Side of Body	Giving out, letting go, masculine energy, men, the father.	*I balance my masculine energy easily and effortlessly.*
Ringworm	Allowing others to get under your skin. Not feeling good enough or clean enough.	*I love and approve of myself. No person, place or thing has any power over me. I am free.*
Root Canal See: Teeth	Can't bite into anything anymore. Root beliefs being destroyed.	*I create firm foundations for myself and for my life. I choose my beliefs to support me joyously.*

Round Shoulders
See: Shoulders,
Spinal Curvature

Carrying the burdens of life. Helpless and hopeless.

I stand tall and free. I love and approve of me. My life gets better every day.

Sagging Lines

Sagging lines on the face come from sagging thoughts in the mind. Resentment of life.

I express the joy of living and allow myself to enjoy every moment of every day totally. I become young again.

Scabies

Infected thinking. Allowing others to get under your skin.

I am the living, loving, joyous expression of life. I am my own person.

Sciatica

Being hypocritical. Fear of money and of the future.

I move into my greater good. My good is everywhere, and I am secure and safe.

Scleroderma

Protecting the self from life. Not trusting yourself to be there and to take care of yourself.

I relax completely for I now know I am safe. I trust Life and I trust myself.

Scoliosis
See: Round Shoulders,
Spinal Curvature

61

Scratches	Feeling life tears at you, that life is a ripoff. That you are being ripped off.	I am grateful for life's generosity to me. I am blessed.
Seasickness See: Motion Sickness	Fear. Fear of death. Lack of control.	I am totally safe in the Universe. I am at peace everywhere. I trust Life.
Seizures	Running away from the family, from the self, or from life.	I am at home in the universe. I am safe and secure and understood.
Senility See: Alzheimer's Disease	Returning to the so-called safety of childhood. Demanding care and attention. A form of control of those around you. Escapism.	*Divine protection. Safety. Peace. The Intelligence of the Universe operates at every level of life.*
Shin(s)	Breaking down ideals. Shins represent the standards of life.	I live up to my highest standards with love and with joy.
Shingles (Varicella)	Waiting for the other shoe to drop. Fear and tension. Too sensitive.	I am relaxed and peaceful because I trust the process of life. All is well in my world.
Shoulders See: Joints, Round Shoulders	Represent our ability to carry our experiences in life joyously. We make life a burden by our attitude.	I choose to allow all my experiences to be joyous and loving.

Sickle Cell Anemia	A belief that one is not good enough that destroys the very joy of life.	*This child lives and breathes the joy of life and is nourished by love. God works miracles every day.*
Sinus Problems (Sinusitis)	Irritation to one person, someone close.	*I declare peace and harmony indwell me and surround me at all times. All is well.*
Skeleton See: Bones	Crumbling of structure. Bones represent the structure of your life.	*I am strong and sound. I am well structured.*
Skin	Protects our individuality. A sense organ.	*I feel safe to be me.*
Skin Problems See: Hives, Psoriasis, Rash	Anxiety, fear. Old, buried guck. I am being threatened.	*I lovingly protect myself with thoughts of joy and peace. The past is forgiven and forgotten. I am free in this moment.*
Slipped Disc	Feeling totally unsupported by Life. Indecisive.	*Life supports all of my thoughts; therefore, I love and approve of myself and all is well.*
Snoring	Stubborn refusal to let go of old patterns.	*I release all that is unlike love and joy in my mind. I move from the past into the new and fresh and vital.*

Solar Plexus	Gut reactions. Center of our intuitive power.	*I trust my inner voice. I am strong, wise and powerful.*
Sore Throat See: Quinsy, Throat, Tonsillitis	Holding in angry words. Feeling unable to express the self.	*I release all restrictions and I am free to be me.*
Sores	Unexpressed anger that settles in.	*I express my emotions in joyous, positive ways.*
Spasms	Tightening our thoughts through fear.	*I release, I relax and I let go. I am safe in life.*
Spastic Colitis See: Colitis, Colon, Intestines, Mucus Colon	Fear of letting go. Insecurity.	*It is safe for me to live. Life will always provide for me. All is well.*
Spinal Curvature **(Scoliosis Kyphosis)** See: Round Shoulders, Spinal Misalignments: Special Section, Page 74	The inability to flow with the support of Life. Fear and trying to hold on to old ideas. Not trusting life. Lack of integrity. No courage of convictions.	*I release all fears. I now trust the process of life. I know that life is for me. I stand straight and tall with love.*

Spinal Meningitis	Inflamed thinking and rage at life.	*I release all blame and accept the peacefulness and joy of life.*
Spine See: Spinal Mis- alignments: Special Section, Page 74	Flexible support of life.	*I am supported by Life.*
Spleen	Obsessions. Being obsessed about things.	*I love and approve of myself. I trust the process of life to be there for me. I am safe. All is well.*
Sprains	Anger and resistance. Not wanting to move in a certain direction in life.	*I trust the process of life to take me only to my highest good. I am at peace.*
Sterility	Fear and resistance to the process of life, OR not needing to go through the parenting experience.	*I trust in the process of life. I am always in the right place, doing the right things, at the right time. I love and approve of myself.*
Stiff Neck See: Neck Problems	Unbending bullheadedness.	*It is safe to see other viewpoints.*
Stiffness	Rigid, stiff thinking.	*I am safe enough to be flexible in my mind.*

Stomach	Holds nourishment. Digests ideas.	I digest life with ease.
Stomach Problems See: Gastritis, Heartburn, Peptic Ulcer, Ulcers	Dread. Fear of the new. Inability to assimilate the new.	Life agrees with me. I assimilate the new every moment of every day. All is well.
Stroke (Cerebrovascular Accident/CVA)	Giving up. Resistance. "Rather die than change." Rejection of life.	Life is change, and I adapt easily to the new. I accept life – past, present and future.
Stuttering	Insecurity. Lack of self-expression. Not being allowed to cry.	I am free to speak up for myself. I am now secure in my own expression. I communicate only with love.
Sty See: Eye Problems	Looking at life through angry eyes. Angry at someone.	I choose to see everyone and everything with joy and love.
Suicide	See life only in black and white. Refusal to see another way out.	I live in the totality of possibilities. There is always another way. I am safe.
Swelling See: Edema, Holding Fluids	Being stuck in thinking. Clogged, painful ideas.	My thoughts flow freely and easily. I move through ideas with ease.

Syphilis
See: Venereal Disease

Tapeworm

Teeth

−Problems
See: Root Canal

**Temporomandibular
Joint**
See: Jaw Problems

Testicles

Tetanus
See: Lockjaw

Giving away your power and effectiveness.

Strong belief in being a victim and unclean. Helpless to the seeming attitudes of others.

Represent decisions.

Longstanding indecisiveness. Inability to break down ideas for analysis and decisions.

Masculine principle. Masculinity.

A need to release angry, festering thoughts.

I decide to be me. I approve of myself as I am.

Others only reflect the good feelings I have about myself. I love and approve of all that I am.

I make my decisions based on the principles of truth, and I rest securely knowing that only right action is taking place in my life.

It is safe to be a man.

I allow the love from my own heart to wash through me and cleanse and heal every part of my body and my emotions.

Throat	Avenue of expression. Channel of creativity.	*I open my heart and sing the joys of love.*
– Problems See: Sore Throat	The inability to speak up for one's self. Swallowed anger. Stifled creativity. Refusal to change.	*It's okay to make noise, I express myself freely and joyously. I speak up for myself with ease. I express my creativity. I am willing to change.*
Thrush See: Candida, Mouth, Yeast Infections	Anger over making the *wrong* decisions.	*I lovingly accept my decisions, knowing I am free to change. I am safe.*
Thymus	Master gland of the immune system. Feeling attacked by Life. *They are* out to get me.	*My loving thoughts keep my immune system strong. I am safe inside and out. I hear myself with love.*
Thyroid See: Goiter, Hyperthyroidism, Hypothyroidism	Humiliation. "I never get to do what I want to do. When is it going to be my turn?"	*I move beyond old limitations and now allow myself to express freely and creatively.*
Tics, Twitches	Fear. A feeling of being watched by others.	*I am approved of by all of Life. All is well. I am safe.*

Tinnitus	Refusal to listen. Not hearing the inner voice. Stubbornness.	*I trust my Higher Self. I listen with love to my inner voice. I release all that is unlike the action of love.*
Toes	Represent the minor details of the future.	*All details take care of themselves.*
Tongue	Represents the ability to taste the pleasures of life with joy.	*I rejoice in all of my life's bountiful givingness.*
Tonsillitis See: Quinsy, Sore Throat	Fear. Repressed emotions. Stifled creativity.	*My good now flows freely. Divine ideas express through me. I am at peace.*
Tuberculosis	Wasting away from selfishness. Possessive. Cruel thoughts. Revenge.	*As I love and approve of myself, I create a joyful, peaceful world to live in.*
Tumors	Nursing old hurts and shocks. Build-ing remorse.	*I lovingly release the past and turn my attention to this new day. All is well.*
Ulcers See: Heartburn, Peptic Ulcer, Stomach Problems	Fear. A strong belief that you are not good enough. What is eating away at you?	*I love and approve of myself. I am at peace. I am calm. All is well.*

Urethritis

Angry emotions. Being pissed off. Blame.

I only create joyful experiences in my life.

Urinary Infections (Cystitis, Pyelonephritis)

Pissed off. Usually at the opposite sex or a lover. Blaming others.

I release the pattern in my consciousness that created this condition. I am willing to change. I love and approve of myself.

Urticaria See:Hives

Uterus

Represents the home of creativity.

I am at home in my body.

Vaginitis See: Female Problems, Leukorrhea

Anger at a mate. Sexual guilt. Punishing the self.

Others mirror the love and self-approval I have for myself. I rejoice in my sexuality.

Varicella See: Shingles

Varicose Veins

Standing in a situation you hate. Discouragement. Feeling overworked and overburdened.

I stand in truth and live and move in joy. I love Life, and circulate freely.

70

Vasovagal Attack
See: Fainting

Venereal Disease
See: AIDS, Gonor-
rhea, Herpes, Syphilis

Sexual guilt. Need for punishment.
Belief that the genitals are sinful or
dirty. Abusing another.

*I lovingly and joyously accept my
sexuality and its expression. I accept
only thoughts that support me and
make me feel good.*

Vertigo
See: Dizziness

Viral Infections
See: Infection

Lack of joy flowing through life.
Bitterness.

*I lovingly allow joy to flow freely in
my life. I love me.*

Vitiligo

Feeling completely outside of things.
Not belonging. Not one of the group.

*I am at the very center of Life, and I
am totally connected in Love.*

Vomiting

Violent rejection of ideas. Fear of the
new.

*I digest life safely and joyously. Only
good comes to me and through me.*

Vulva

Represents vulnerability.

It is safe to be vulnerable.

Warts

Little expressions of hate. Belief in
ugliness.

*I am the love and the beauty of Life
in full expression.*

71

Weakness	A need for mental rest.	*I give my mind a joyous vacation.*
Whiteheads See: Pimples	Hiding ugliness.	*I accept myself as beautiful and loved.*
Widsom Tooth, Impacted	Not giving yourself mental space to create a firm foundation.	*I open my consciousness to the expansion of life. There is plenty of space for me to grow and to change.*
Wounds See: Cuts, Injuries	Anger and guilt at the self.	*I forgive myself and I choose to love myself.*
Wrist	Represents movement and ease.	*I handle all my experiences with wisdom, with love, and with ease.*
Yeast Infections See: Candida, Thrush	Denying your own needs. Not supporting yourself.	*I now choose to support myself in loving, joyous ways.*

SPECIAL SECTION
SPINAL MISALIGNMENTS

So many people have back problems that are so diversified that I felt it would be helpful to list the spine and all the vertebrae as a separate category. Please study the accompanying spinal chart with its information. Then cross-reference the chart with the mental equivalents listed below. As always, use your own wisdom to ascertain the meaning that is most helpful to you.

CHART OF EFFECTS OF SPINAL MISALIGNMENTS

Vertebrae	Areas	Effects
1C	Blood supply to the head, pituitary gland, scalp, bones of the face, brain, inner and middle ear, sympathetic nervous system.	Headaches, nervousness, insomnia, head colds, high blood pressure, migraine headaches, nervous breakdowns, amnesia, chronic tiredness, dizziness.
2C	Eyes, optic nerves, auditory nerves, sinuses, mastoid bones, tongue, forehead.	Sinus trouble, allergies, crossed eyes, deafness, eye troubles, earache, fainting spells, certain cases of blindness.
3C	Cheeks, outer ear, face bones, teeth, trifacial nerve.	Neuralgia, neuritis, acne or pimples, eczema.
4C	Nose, lips, mouth, eustachian tube.	Hay fever, catarrh, hearing loss, adenoids.
5C	Vocal cords, neck glands, pharynx.	Laryngitis, hoarseness, throat conditions such as sore throat or quinsy.
6C	Neck muscles, shoulders, tonsils.	Stiff neck, pain in upper arm, tonsillitis, whooping cough, croup.
7C	Thyroid gland, bursae in the shoulders, elbows.	Bursitis, colds, thyroid conditions.
1T	Arms from the elbows down, including hands, wrists, and fingers; esophagus and trachea.	Asthma, cough, difficult breathing, shortness of breath, pain in lower arms and hands.
2T	Heart, including its valves and covering; coronary arteries	Functional heart conditions and certain chest conditions.
3T	Lungs, bronchial tubes, pleura, chest, breast.	Bronchitis, pleurisy, pneumonia, congestion, influenza.
4T	Gall bladder, common duct.	Gall bladder conditions, jaundice, shingles.
5T	Liver, solar plexus, blood.	Liver conditions, fevers, low blood pressure, anemia, poor circulation, arthritis.
6T	Stomach.	Stomach troubles, including nervous stomach, indigestion, heartburn, dyspepsia.

ATLAS
AXIS
CERVICAL SPINE
1st THORACIC

NECK REGION

MID-BACK

THORACIC SPINE

Vertebra	Structures/Organs	Conditions
7T	Pancreas, duodenum.	Ulcers, gastritis.
8T	Spleen.	Lowered resistance.
9T	Adrenal and supra-renal glands.	Allergies, hives.
10T	Kidneys.	Kidney troubles, hardening of the arteries, chronic tiredness, nephritis, pyelitis.
11T	Kidneys, ureters.	Skin conditions such as acne, pimples, eczema, or boils.
12T	Small intestines, lymph circulation.	Rheumatism, gas pains, certain types of sterility.
1L	Large intestines, inguinal rings.	Constipation, colitis, dysentery, diarrhea, some ruptures or hernias.
2L	Appendix, abdomen, upper leg.	Cramps, difficult breathing, acidosis, varicose veins.
3L	Sex organs, uterus, bladder, knees.	Bladder troubles, menstrual troubles such as painful or irregular periods, miscarriages, bed wetting, impotency, change of life symptoms, many knee pains.
4L	Prostate gland, muscles of the lower back, sciatic nerve.	Sciatica: lumbago; difficult, painful, or too frequent urination; backaches.
5L	Lower legs, ankles, feet.	Poor circulation in the legs, swollen ankles, weak ankles and arches, cold feet, weakness in the legs, leg cramps.
SACRUM	Hip bones, buttocks.	Sacro-iliac conditions, spinal curvatures.
COCCYX	Rectum, anus.	Hemorrhoids (piles), pruritis (itching), pain at end of spine on sitting.

1st LUMBAR
LUMBAR SPINE
SACRUM
COCCYX

LOW BACK
PELVIS

Misalignments of spinal vertebrae and discs may cause irritation to the nervous system and affect the structures, organs, and functions which may result in the conditions shown above.

75

SPINAL MISALIGNMENTS

VERTEBRAE	PROBABLE CAUSE	NEW THOUGHT PATTERN
Cervical Spine		
1-C	Fear. Confusion. Running from life. Feeling not good enough. "What will the neighbors say?" Endless inner chatter.	I am centered and calm and balanced. The Universe approves of me. I trust my Higher Self. All is well.
2-C	Rejection of wisdom. Refusal to know or understand. Indecision. Resentment and blame. Out of balance with life. Denial of one's spirituality.	I am one with the Universe and all of life. It is safe for me to know and to grow.
3-C	Accepting blame for others. Guilt. Martyrhood. Indecision. Grinding one's self down. Biting off more than one can chew.	I am responsible only for myself and I rejoice in who I am. I can handle all that I create.

	Problem	Affirmation
4-C	Guilt. Repressed anger. Bitterness. Bottled-up feelings. Stuffed tears.	I am clear in my communication with life. I am free to enjoy life right now.
5-C	Fear of ridicule and humiliation. Fear of expression. Rejecting one's good. Overburdened.	My communication is clear. I accept my good. I let go of all expectations. I am loved and I am safe.
6-C	Burdens. Overload. Trying to fix others. Resistance. Inflexibility.	I lovingly release others to their own lessons. I lovingly care for myself. I move with ease through life.
7-C	Confusion. Anger. Feeling helpless. Can't reach out.	I have a right to be me. I forgive the past. I know who I am. I touch others with love.

Thoracic Spine

	Problem	Affirmation
1-T	Fear of life. Too much to cope with. Can't handle it. Closing off from life.	I accept life and I take it in easily. All good is mine now.
2-T	Fear, pain and hurt. Unwillingness to feel. Shutting the heart off.	My heart forgives and releases. It is safe to love myself. Inner peace is my goal.

3-T	Inner chaos. Deep, old hurts. Inability to communicate.	I forgive everyone. I forgive myself. I nourish myself.
4-T	Bitterness. A need to make others wrong. Condemnation.	I give myself the gift of forgiveness and we are both free.
5-T	Refusing to process the emotions. Dammed-up feelings, rage.	I let life flow through me. I am willing to live. All is well.
6-T	Anger at life. Stuffed negative emotions. Fear of the future. Constant worry.	I trust life to unfold before me in positive ways. It is safe to love myself.
7-T	Storing pain. Refusal to enjoy.	I willingly let go. I allow sweetness to fill my life.
8-T	Obsession with failure. Resisting your good.	I am open and receptive to all good. The Universe loves me and supports me.
9-T	Feeling let down by life. Blaming others. A victim.	I claim my own power. I lovingly create my own reality.
10-T	Refusal to take charge. Needing to be a victim. "It's your fault."	I open myself to joy and love, which I give freely and receive freely.

11-T	Low self-image. Fear of relationships.	*I see myself as beautiful and loveable and appreciated. I am proud to be me.*
12-T	Disowning the right to live. Insecure and fearful of love. Inability to digest.	*I choose to circulate the joys of life. I am willing to nourish myself.*

Lumbar Spine

1-L	A crying for love and a need to be lonely. Insecurity.	*I am safe in the universe and all Life loves me and supports me.*
2-L	Stuck in childhood pain. See no way out.	*I grow beyond my parents' limitations and live for myself. It is my turn now.*
3-L	Sexual abuse. Guilt. Self-hatred.	*I release the past. I cherish myself and my beautiful sexuality. I am safe. I am loved.*
4-L	Rejection of sexuality. Financial insecurity. Fear of career. Feeling powerless.	*I love who I am. I am grounded in my own power. I am secure on all levels.*

79

5-L	Insecurity. Difficulty in communicating. Anger. Inability to accept pleasure.	*I deserve to enjoy life. I ask for what I want and I accept with joy and pleasure.*
Sacrum	Loss of power. Old stubborn anger.	*I am the power and authority in my life. I release the past and claim my good now.*
Coccyx	Out of balance with yourself. Holding on. Blame of self. Sitting on old pain.	*I bring my life into balance by loving myself. I live in today and love who I am*

FURTHER COMMENTS

I have learned that children, and animals too, because they are so open, may be largely influenced by the consciousness of the adults around them. Therefore, when working for children or pets, use the affirmations both for them and for also clearing the consciousness of the parent, teacher, relative, etc. who may be surrounding and influencing them.

Remember, the word *metaphysical* means to go beyond the physical to the mental cause behind it. As an example, if you came to me as a client with a problem of constipation, I would know you had some sort of belief in limitation and lack and, therefore, were mentally frightened to let go of anything out of fear of not being able to replace it. It could also mean you were holding onto an old, painful memory of the past and would not let go. You might have a fear of letting go of relationships that no longer nourish you, or a job that is unfulfilling, or some possessions that are now unusable. You might even be stingy about money. Your dis-ease would give me many clues to your mental attitude.

I would try to make you understand that a closed fist and a tight attitude cannot take in anything new. I would help you develop more trust in the Universe (that power that supplies your breath) to provide for you so that you could flow with the rhythms of life. I would help you to release your patterns of fear and teach you how to create a new cycle of good experiences by using your mind in a different way. I might ask you to go home and clean out your closets, giving away all the useless stuff to make room for new things. And as you were doing this to say aloud, "I am releasing the old and making room for the new." Simple, but effective. And as you began to understand the principle of release and letting go, the constipation, which is a form of gripping and holding on, would take care of itself. The body would freely release that which was no longer useful in a normal way.

Perhaps you have noticed how often I have used the concepts of LOVE, PEACE, JOY and SELF-APPROVAL. When we can truly live from the loving space of the heart, approving of ourselves and trusting the Divine Power to provide for us, then peace and joy will fill our lives and illness and uncomfortable experiences will cease to be in our experience. Our goal is to live happy, healthy lives, enjoying our own company. Love dissolves anger, love releases resentment, love dissipates fear, love creates safety. When you can come from a space of totally loving yourself, then everything in your life must flow with ease and harmony and health and prosperity and joy.

A good way to use this book when you have a physical problem;

1. Look up the mental cause. See if this could be true for you. If not, sit quietly and ask yourself, "What could be the thoughts in me that created this?"
2. Repeat to yourself (aloud if you can), "I am willing to release the pattern in my consciousness that has created this condition."

3. Repeat the new thought pattern to yourself several times.
4. Assume that you are already in the process of healing.

Whenever you think of the condition, repeat the steps.

This closing meditation is helpful to read daily as it creates a healthy consciousness and, therefore, a healthy body.

LOVING TREATMENT

DEEP AT THE CENTER OF MY BEING, there is an infinite well of love. I now allow this love to flow to the surface. It fills my heart, my body, my mind, my consciousness, my very being, and radiates out from me in all directions and returns to me multiplied. The more love I use and give, the more I have to give, the supply is endless. The use of love makes ME FEEL GOOD, it is an expression of my inner joy. I love myself; therefore, I take loving care of my body. I lovingly feed it nourishing foods and beverages, I lovingly groom it and dress it, and my body lovingly responds to me with vibrant health and energy. I love myself; therefore, I provide for myself a comfortable home, one that fills all my needs and is a pleasure to be in. I fill the rooms with the vibration of love so that all who enter, myself included, will feel this love and be nourished by it.

I love myself; therefore, I work at a job that I truly enjoy doing, one that uses my creative talents and abilities, working with and for people that I love and that love me, and earning a good income. I love myself; therefore, I behave and think in a loving way to all people, for I know that that which I give out returns to me multiplied. I only attract loving people in my world, for they are a mirror of what I am. I love myself; therefore, I forgive and totally release the past and all past experiences and I am free. I love myself; therefore, I live totally in the now, experiencing each moment as good and knowing that my future is bright and joyous and secure, for I am a beloved child of the universe and the universe lovingly takes care of me now and forever more. And, so it is.

I love you.

Louise L. Hay, author of the best-selling book, *You Can Heal Your Life,* is an internationally-renown counselor, teacher and lecturer.

Dr. Hay's key message is "If we are willing to the mental work, almost anything can be healed." The author has a great deal of experience and first-hand information about the mental patterns that create physical illness including her own self healing from cancer. In her frequent lectures, workshops and training programs, Dr. Hay offers practical steps for dissolving both the fears and the causations of diseases. She devotes her life to assisting others in discovering and using the full potential of their own creative powers.

BOOKS AND AUDIO TAPES BY LOUISE L. HAY

Books

The AIDS Book: Creating A Positive Approach
Colors & Numbers
Heal Your Body
Heart Thoughts: A Treasury of Inner Wisdom
A Garden of Thoughts: My Affirmation Journal
Love Yourself, Heal Your Life Workbook
Love Your Body
The Power is Within You
You Can Heal Your Life

Coloring Books/Audios for Children

Lulu and the Ant: A Message of Love
Lulu and the Dark: Conquering Fears
Lulu and Willy the Duck: Learning Mirror Work

Audio Tapes

AIDS: A Positive Approach
Cancer: Discovering Your Healing Power
Feeling Fine Affirmations
Gift of the Present with Joshua Leeds
Heal Your Body Book on Tape
Love Your Body Book on Tape
Loving Yourself
Morning and Evening Meditations
Overcoming Fears
Self Healing
Songs of Affirmation with Joshua Leeds
What I Believe / Deep Relaxation
You Can Heal Your Life Study Course
You Can Heal Your Life Book on Tape

Conversations on Living Lecture Series

Change and Transition
Dissolving Barriers
The Forgotten Child Within
How to Love Yourself
The Power of Your Spoken Word
Receiving Prosperity
Totality of Possibilities
Your Thoughts Create Your Life

Personal Power Through Imagery Series

Anger Releasing
Forgiveness/Loving the Inner Child

Subliminal Mastery Series

Feeling Fine Affirmations
Love Your Body Affirmations
Safe Driving Affirmations
Self-Esteem Affirmations
Self-Healing Affirmations
Stress-Free Affirmations

For free catalog, call 1-800-654-5126